CITYSCAPE

Tirtho

Leadstart
INKSTATE

ISBN 978-93-90040-22-3
Copyright © Tirtho, 2020

First published in India 2021 by Leadstart Inkstate
A Division of One Point Six Technologies Pvt Ltd

Sales Office:
Unit No.25/26, Building No.A/1,
Near Wadala RTO,
Wadala (East), Mumbai – 400037 India
Phone: +91 969933000
Email: info@leadstartcorp.com
www.leadstartcorp.com

Disclaimer: The views expressed in this book are those of the Author and do not pertain to be held by the Publisher.

Editor: Vaibhav Pathare
Cover: Ashwini Jadhav
Layouts: Kshitij Dhawale

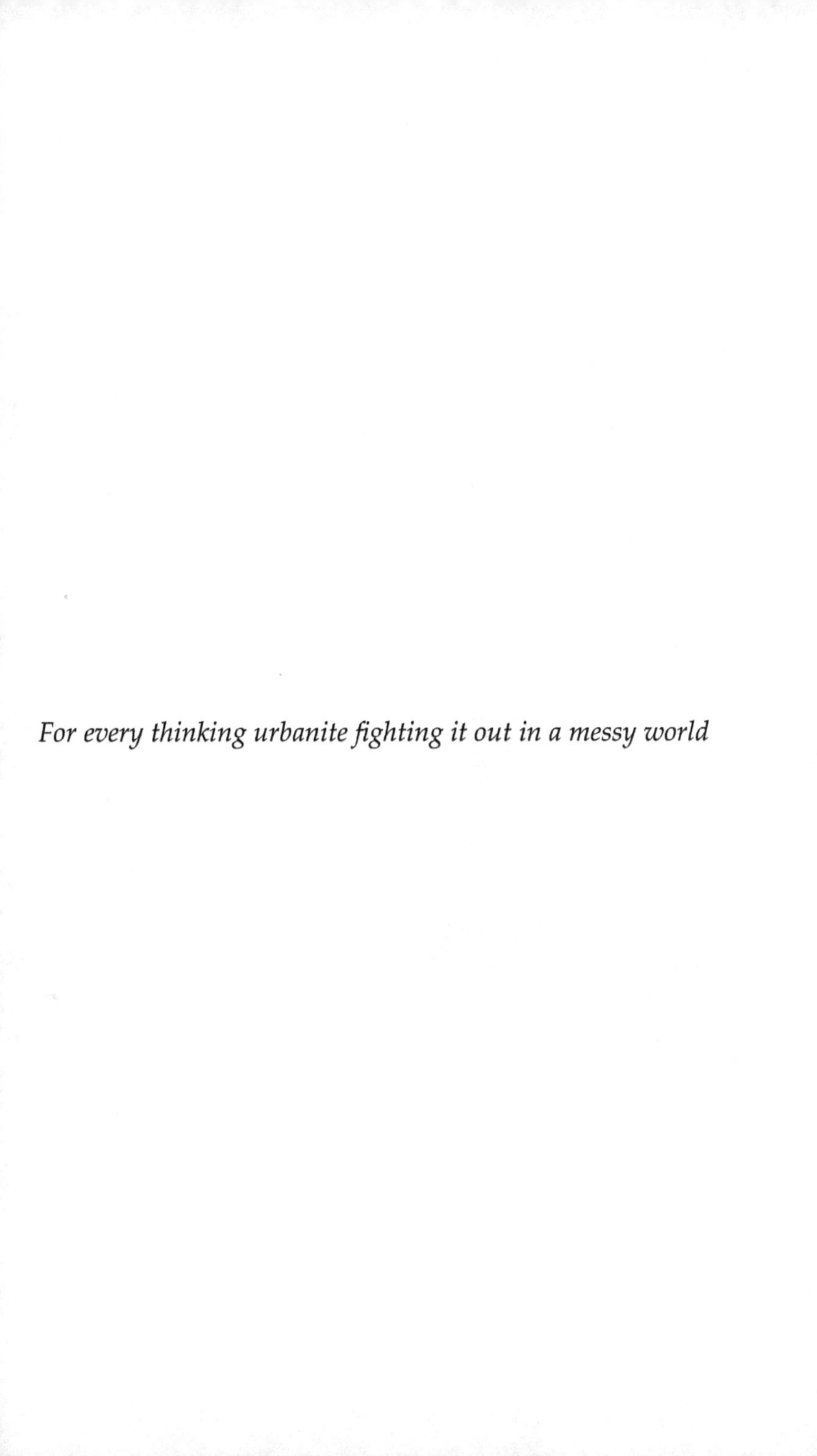

For every thinking urbanite fighting it out in a messy world

Contents

About the Author

Acknowledgements

This book wouldn't have happened if I hadn't closely seen and deeply felt the challenges of living in the urban milieu. The inspiration often came from random mundane incidents and stray experiences which made an imprint on my mind.

My gratitude goes out to my wife, Tuhina, for her unflinching support; my mother, Shibani, for being there every time I faltered; my father, Ram Chandra, for praising my sometimes 'incomprehensible' words; my kids, Neil and Rishyap, for being patient with their 'crazy' dad; my brother, Partho, and my sisters, Chandana and Moushumi, who always showered trust on me when I needed it the most.

Deepest thanks to all my friends, including those on Facebook and Instagram, and well-wishers whose appreciation and 'Likes' gave me a reason to keep scribbling. I am indebted to each one of you out there who egged me on to articulate my thoughts, even when I was unsure of my expressions. A big thanks to all the critics, who helped me plug the loopholes and go the extra mile.

I am grateful to Leadstart Publishing, whose team is like a family now. I wish to thank every member of the Leadstart team for turning my dream into reality.

Urban Truth

We have become cities…

Our dreams high-rises
which feel the morning haze.

Our hearts swanky malls
which are always abuzz, but lonely.

Our ambitions crawling cars
which pollute our innocence.

Our thoughts Metro trains
which run only between fixed destinations.

Our bodies urban landscapes
which erode our souls.

Wow! City Life

Wow! what a city life…

where everything is set on fast track
but trust is slow to come,

where every smile that flickers on lips
has a teary tale to tell,

where distances are covered each day
but gaps grow between hearts and remain unbridged,

where firm handshakes and emphatic hellos
are too frail to go beyond the ritual,

where everyday targets and deadlines
blur the real goal,

where we exist with our wants
but have forgotten what we need most.

— Virtual World —

With her head down
and her eyes glued
to her smartphone,
she made no eye contact
with the real world.

Perhaps, she saw those
people too complicated, tangled
and found refuge
in her 'web'.

●———— *No Spoken Word* ————●

Sometimes, I wonder
what if all the people stop speaking?
The spoken words fall silent.
There's no conversation,
no vocal vibrations!

We say what we want to and voice our feelings
only through written words.
Will they sound the same way?
Create the same impact?

Blessings

Wishes come with a click of a button,
blessings don't...

— Terror Goes Viral —

There was a time when a smile went viral.

Now, it hardly does.

There are tears, tragedies, agonies and terrors
that are more infectious today.

—— ● —— *Pickpocket* —— ● ——

He stole a pocketful of trust,
not just my wallet.

— Carbon Tale —

Your car is really sexy and hot,
It melts the coolest one — The Glaciers.

Acid Of Distrust

The scar on her face would heal
but the toxic wound in her soul would last forever.
The acid of distrust will burn it little by little.

Chain Of Distrust

It's a chain of distrust
that makes the world suffer.
Break it and most ills will evaporate.

Job

Half of your life is lost
in finding a foothold in a job.
Half of it is spent in saving it.
And in all this, the joy of enjoying
the work gets lost.

Starved Humanity

This progress with a hollow halo around it
won't last too long.
This civilization
which can't feed on reality
will starve mankind.

Torrent Of Technology

The torrent of technology
sweeps civilization away.

 Sabotage

These fake faiths, pseudo prayers
can't get you near to the divine power you call God.

Cosmetic chants make
you unworthy of nirvana you frenziedly seek.

The unreality of your worship
is what sabotages your salvation.

— Give Gods A Break —

Break illusions of
hallowed places,
their false sacredness.

Debunk the pseudo piety,
myths of divinity in the walls
that house profanity.

Stop declaring sanctity
in the pealing of the jarring bells
that ring hollow
and can't drown the loud hypocrisy.

Do away with those manufactured mantras,
those rants that spell deception.

Let the temples sleep
and give Gods a break.

Back To Zero

This numbers game
drives the competition
and then the counting stops at zero!

 Budget

The monthly dilemma
that throws us into a predicament
to set ugly priorities...
Hobson's choices!

—— Biggest Scam ——

This world is a big-time scam;
its ways cheat us;
we cry foul, but continue to be conned.

Concrete Forest

The moon vanishes somewhere
and the sun emerges from nowhere.

Haze

My eyes saw
in the haze, an uncontaminated truth
with blinding clarity:
We are doomed.

Struggle

419—they said,
with dismay writ in their eyes.
Back in 2014,
I hardly knew
what the count meant,
until it sunk in like the insidious pain of the sting.

They imposed a change on my taste buds,
and caps on the tongue's propensities too...
(I felt too powerless to cringe or protest)
but how could I change the temperament lying deep?
The blood couldn't stop seething at the 'dark' sights
and the dancing vein kept up its battle to emote.

This lonely run continues,
the sugary swings have steadied me.
I am more aware; the helplessness is wise.
The endless journey of 'one touches' has brought me
closer to the deep, inner chaos of my body
so I can embrace the silence of my spirit, someday...

— Nowhere Road —

We all are mental wrecks
running on a long-winding path
that takes us nowhere.
The slightly saner ones
have shut themselves up in their rooms.

Bed Bugs

Bed bugs sucked.
Robbed of sleep,
I hunted them wherever I could
and squashed many, almost all.
And then watched the blood, my blood!

I changed my room,
the bed, the bed sheets...
till I knew there were none left.
I did everything to shun those parasites.
But the fear of being bitten
clung to me.

I still feel being bitten,
I scratch the rashes
that are no more there.
I feel one of them crawling over me.
It's the paranoia...
which I try to get rid of.
Will I ever?

Worm Inside A Monitor

It got inside from somewhere, nowhere
and seemed to enjoy the adventure
till it found itself trapped in the escapade.

The worm lost its way out
as it wriggled hard
to embrace the world it had left
to be free again!

In A Taxi

A muggy morning,
sweat sticking to my favourite shirt,
enticing smell of the Ethiopian coffee
floating in the taxi.
The cabbie driving me to the Metro station,
a woman's voice from a faraway town
wearing off on the mobile phone,
faint memory of cuddling a baby
frozen in a treasured snap,
eyes hiding a helpless agony
with a coaxed out smile,
a living unworthy of
the inescapable grind.

Greens' Quandary

What will the pseudo eco-warriors do
as pollution becomes increasingly business-friendly?
Will they hold meetings to find ways
to befriend the thriving community?

Indigenous Is Intelligent

Turmoil in the soil
and menace of a hybrid race.

# *Hybrid*

This hybrid generation
sucks more energy to grow.

Regret

I started early—really early,
but got caught up in the traffic snarls.
The red signals seemed to stay that way
more than they used to usually.
Through every bottleneck,
I risked negotiating my chaotic way
without caring about the rules.
I tried many shortcuts, almost unmindful of the speedometer.
But I still reached late.
Maybe, 15 minutes or so.

You had left
perhaps, waiting for me, desperately
till your eyes turned stony
and you felt all eyes riveted on you.
Tired, embarrassed... you gave up the wait.

I looked for you everywhere, frantically.
Asked the chaiwalaa who had once given us tea
in an earthen cup, when we had insisted to be served like that.
That routine beggar who had blessed us
when we had offered him some loose change (alms)
just to ensure he doesn't pester us.

But they had not noticed you standing there.

I came back downcast.

Yes, I was late
and you had every right to punish me for my offence,
but wasn't parting a price too dear?

No, I don't blame you for anything,
since I know love needs to be punctual. It should have a sense of time.
But I have only one regret.
I couldn't tell you that
I had started really early,
it was the only thing in my control, others were not.
I wished we had met that day
and decided on taking a road
where there would have been no traffic, no red signals,
no waiting and no misunderstanding at all.

Pram Fever

They can't wait to
see the babys' first steps
and then put them in prams
with the same hurry.

— After A Terror Attack —

I don't know what resilience is...
Is it to show a semblance
of an endurance to bear an unbearable pain?

Self-Consolation Expires

We have a tendency to appease ourselves
looking at those who are worse off than us
at the workplace, home or elsewhere.
We call this self-consolation—
a forced ease to stay happy.
We forget that self-consolation has an expiry date
but dissatisfaction doesn't.
The disgruntled heart will always strike again
and itch for something new and more… every time
after the self-consolation wanes.

—— *Munching Chips* ——

It often happens that you find
some potato chips so irresistible
that you keep munching
till your hand comes out empty from the packet.

Some desires are so engaging
that you do not worry about overindulging in them
till you realize how they have blanked your heart.

Privacy Blues

The porous walls
couldn't withstand
the moans!

●——— *Imagination Liberates* ——●

Don't bust all truths
with staid science and dull logic.
Let the romance of a rainbow stay
and the fun of an intriguing Santa remain.
Imagination is liberating
and overload of reality stifles.

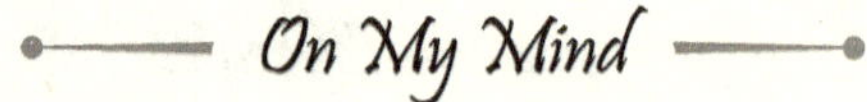

— *On My Mind* —

Why has our conscience lost its spine?
Why are we too broken to piece ourselves together?
Why do we regret, but go on doing what we do?
Are we slaves of a tyrant acceptance?
Are we preys of our own misplaced choices?

Smiles And Sleep

Every morning
he woke up half-asleep, bleary-eyed
to wave her bye with a smile
when she took the elevator down...

Every night
she forced herself awake
with sleep-starved eyes
to greet him with a smile
as he stepped in.

It were their smiles
that made up for their lost sleep.

 **_Illusion_**

Two Metro trains stop beside each other
going in opposite directions.
Images overlap and some are half-formed.
It seems we all are swapping our places, partly
but actually, we don't.
We stay where we are,
only illusion positions us otherwise.

—— *Lost Footwear* ——

He lost his new footwear;
someone stole the shoes
when he left them at the shrine door.

He felt embarrassed to go barefoot,
He looked around
and settled for a slipper—which looked new—
lying among the heaps.
It was a mismatch, though
and it did hurt a bit.

He wondered whose it was,
And did the one who wore his - fit the guy?
Will the guy ever know how it felt when he wore
the brand new thing for the first time?
Will the guy ever realize how it felt to lose one?

He put the slipper back in the pile of shoes
And came back barefoot...
it was embarrassing, but it didn't hurt him anymore!

Be Real

Your face isn't a PRO
that should force a smile
to please people.

Your heart isn't an ad
that displays and claims
what's not there!

Joke

Civilization cracks a joke on our lofty wisdom
And derides the shallow progress
that blurs the distinction humans boast of.
It belittles our foolish pursuit
of myopically building skyscrapers of logic
on ruins of common sense.

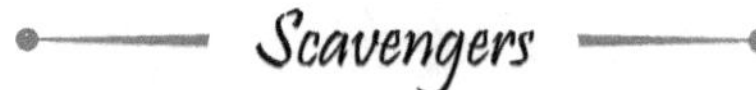 Scavengers

They tried to
unclog the waste
and choked on it.

Post-Win

A tough battle won, at last,
An army of emotions slain.

A flower blooms, finally,
A bud's innocence is lost.

A newfound joy glimmers,
A shadow lingers.

A pride marches,
A virtue retreats.

A veil is lifted,
A truth is masked.

A gift is dished out,
A hunger is snatched.

— **Futile Chase** —

Our cities are mirages
which leave us more thirsty.
We get sucked into
the infiniteness of illusions
and give our elusive dreams
a futile chase.

Development Chokes Dreams

The little boy has Messi dreams
but he has no place to play or practice.

The grounds are all gone.
How many more dreams
will this development choke to death?

Self-Identity

Don't be a ship adrift
which is lost in the sea (of humanity)
and doesn't know its shore.

Don't be a dry leaf
on the street, rustling...
seeking vainly its roots.

Don't be an inconsequential mirror
dangling by a nail
which has almost come off the wall.

Credit

We mortgage our breaths
for a borrowed living.

Hacked!

The narrow minds
widened the roads
and took the shade away.

They curse the sun now
and watch the rainless clouds pass by.

——• **Crazy Culture** •——

The fumes of toxic growth
have made them delirious,
They dance and party
lost in a senseless glee.

That 'Beggar'

He faked his pain.
The hurt was not there.
I looked at his face
and yet gave away my sympathy;
Feeling sorry for his make-believe.

—————— Domestic Abuse ——————

The haunting shrieks of pain
invaded their love-making.
She couldn't come
as she failed to get over the cries
of the woman battered by her 'lover'.

Gridlock

Honk horn,
vent your rage,
mouth profanities,
curse your fate,
sweat out in AC,
burn your blood.

But...can you make the
traffic move by these?

— The Divide —

It's a gap
that no earnest talk,
no radical pact, no noble experiment
can ever bridge.

It will stay yawning...
The mouth won't shut
but the stomachs
will only be filled with empty promises.

Floods

It's a city
swamped by
tears of neglect;
a deluge
which brings
the apathy to fore.

Girl At Call Centre

Her mechanized voice
gave away
the phoneyness of her help.

Bottled Up!

We rip the ground
and then sip the mountain water.

—— *Killer Selfie* ——

Life stopped him
on its tracks
and the selfie
made him free.

Escape

This feeling of alienation
roots for an escape
from commodified dreams.

A sense of resignation
screams reluctance
to carry on with the farcical exercise.

In A Red Light Zone

A make-up
too heavy to entice.
Fancy earrings
too bright to allure.
A dress
too exposed to appeal.
A smile
too desperate to invite.

She was taken by three
and yet hadn't the courage to say 'no'.
Age has a price to pay!

— **Tissue Paper** —

A swathe of biodiversity cleared
to clean our bodies.

Monotony

How do we fight monotony?
A question pops up within,
as I see his face.
The office boy collecting
trash from the overflowing bin
in a black single-use plastic bag
and then carrying it to the dumping zone.
He does it every day,
and goes about his act
like a robot...

The banality of his work
clearly uninspires him
but there's hardly any choice.
So, what he does is disengage himself
from his job even as he is fully engaged in it.
Is that possible? I ask myself.
Yes...that's the only way out of the dull regularity
and feel less worn-out.
We can't escape dictates of our routine, mundane grind
which trap us in unchanged patterns of existence.
But we can find a degree of detachment in what we do
that can bring a mindful smile on our face at the workplace.

Jogging At 6:30am

The autistic girl in the park gives it her best
as her parents watch over her movements.
Her jaded eyes look at others
to marvel at the joy that eludes her unfitness.

That 30-something woman at the yoga session
folds up her mat with a smile.
She has to reach her home asap
to save herself another sneer from her in-laws.

An athletic boy on the cycle with his ear phones on,
heedless to the song that the nature sings
and the music that the breeze plays,
only he knows the hum hides his deafness.

A man picking up discarded plastic bottles
crushing them with his hand
to derive a content, vanity...
Then, smoking under a tree
that scoffs at him.

A middle-aged couple lamenting the
shooting inflation, economic slowdown
to give break to their inflated egos
and downslide in their cloyed bonding.

An elderly man sitting on a bench
looking at the rustling dry leaves
with only some withered memories as his company
that want to unmoor his heart.

Are We Liberated?

Are we liberated?
Our thoughts are trapped in false glorifications,
our selfish minds held hostage by insecurities,
our corrupt actions swayed by half lies.

We have become puppets
whose strings are pulled
by the hands of an ambition
that can cut our thread anytime.

Our compromises have made
a chain of shackles,
Our compulsions the ever-growing fetters.
Living in a facade of freedom,
we stay indifferent to our self-made cells,
and can't break the bondage of sham
even when we want to.

No...we are not liberated.

Metropolitans

Foreheads with lines of anxiety shining,
Feet lost in search of a path unknown,
Faces that bear a familiarly strange look,
Bodies bustling in a crowd of chaos,
Hearts strangled by the noose of stress.

They stand in a queue
which follows rules of the daily grind.
They board a train
which has no steam left for fresh journeys,
as the wheels run on tracks
that are too smooth to feel the weariness.

Can We?

Can our adult hearts stay apolitical
with leanings injected into our babyish blood?

Can our undying souls be spiritual
with distorted interpretations of religion swaying our faith?

Can we really love with that selfless devotion
when building a wall of ego is deemed as strength?

Can we want less and still be at peace
while greediness branches its roots into our psyche?

Can fame teach us a lesson in modesty
as it slips out of the hand?

Can we feel the thrill in beauty
as we try to outsmart nature with sordid means?

Can loneliness be more like solitude
which doesn't cage us, but liberates?

Can the truth of an emotion be unveiled
amid hypocrisy of all those masked words?

Can we live a moment of glory
without thinking about the end of an eternity?

Take It, Robot!

OK...
give my job to a robot
if it understands what losing a livelihood means.

If it gets thrilled
when meeting a daily target just to stay afloat in the race .

If it realizes
what toll it takes while constantly trying to outperform.

If it gets let-down
when humiliated for a small lapse despite flawless commitment.

If it gets upset
when pulled up for an inability to put goals before dreams.

If it feels
the reluctance to carry on with the monotony till it becomes a way
of life.

If it knows
what a salary's wait is and how a need propels the heart.

This vacuum of time.
This wounded silence.
This burning darkness.
This echo of the unknown.
This perpetuity of loss.
This wilting flame.
This struggle of conscience.
This demise of a veiled hope.
This city has given me so much to write about.

•——— *Night Makes It Natural* ———•

It's 2:30 am. I am on the 25th floor.
The rumble of those whizzing cars jars my ears,
It sounds like the roar of the sea.

I get up and watch the glimmer of buildings.
They appear like shimmering stars in the sky.

This city has the habit
to become natural
in the dead of the night.

The day holds a different picture.

— Marketplace —

This is a marketplace
where every ambition has a price tag
with an expiry date.
Every stale dream reeks
and then perishes, unseen.

Captives Of Convenience

In the illusions
of embracing freedom,
We have become
captives of convenience.

Space

A lost space of the city
trapped between two skyscrapers
gasps for breath.

It can't live freely
and doesn't want to face
the fate of the buildings that flank it.

There's no escape
from the smothered feeling.

 Quest

A veil of fallacies to justify
the insignificance of a goal
and a smokescreen of pretensions
to cover up an inessential quest.

 *Loss*

We keep up our
relentless fight against nightmares
and battle hard
so our dreams don't defeat us.
And in this effort
of fighting and battling,
we forget the joy of simply drifting into sleep
like a baby.

—— *Chequered Life* ——

We all go about
our self-scripted struggles
entrapped in clockwise arrangements
and chameleon desires
that define the perpetual journey
of our chequered existence.

—— *Mother's Day* ——

Pushed into creches, babies cry.
Their helpless mothers secretly weep
in the unseen corners of workplaces.

Pining For Past

Give me back a wallet-less past
in which there were no
pockets of insecurity.

A cycle of life
whose chain did come off too often
but refused to bother me.

A broken wooden toy
which I pieced together without any fear of being choked,
that gave me a joy nothing else has.

A handwritten letter
whose whiff meandered in memory long after it was read
and was treasured between the pages of a kept-away book.

An earthen pot
whose water slaked my thirst
more than the chilled Cola.

A shirt stitched by a tailor down a familiar street
which sized up well
even if it had a lot of room for fitting.

A cinema hall where
I could break those peanuts and munch on them
giving the dirt a damn, for once.

A transistor which connected me
with my passion and love
through those running cricket commentaries
and songs of oneness on 'Chhaya Geet'.

A prayer chanted in innocence
only to get a modicum of 'prasaad';
but which was deeper than today's 'faith'.

A bed lying on which
I could count the stars
and fall off to sleep.

 *Plot*

The conspiracy of awareness
and the politics of inaction.

Let Me Relive

Let me relive that lost era
when simplicity didn't have wrinkles,
when love was taken at face value, not dissected,
when fun was not swayed by flamboyance,
when a smile was enough to break the ice,
when sharing was a habit, not taught,
when creativity didn't struggle with diffidence,
when journeys were more important than the destinations,

when passion came through spontaneity, not practice,
when follies were seen as ladders to wisdom,
when sunshine fed hopes, not hazard,
when sea absorbed sorrows, not waste,
when power didn't dictate, it taught humility,
when truth wasn't forced to hide its bitterness,
when life was not lived under tyranny of a pyrrhic pleasure.

— Groundless... —

I have no land to call my own,
no roots to anchor my spirit.

The alien air feels me
as I scud like a rainless cloud
without a sky above,
flying like a lost bird who builds nests,
only to be abandoned.

It's a journey of stopovers,
No place belongs to me,
'coz my home is elsewhere!

— *Burnout* —

Exhaustion doesn't come
from the increasing dreariness
of the everyday slog.
It is the fatigue of
a growing frivolity of our toil
that burns us out.

 *Void*

The heart feels heavy
in this growing emptiness of pursuit.
The mind so replete
with the endless void of existence.

—— Death On Road ——

The road was washed with rain.
I was driving slow.
A speeding jeep zipped past me.
In a flash, it swerved and jumped the divider.
There was a thud and then complete silence.

A biker had been smashed.
I saw the jeep's driver escaping.
The dead body was bundled into an ambulance.
The man who died was a sports teacher.
He was agile and fit. No, he didn't deserve such a death.

Next day, while passing by that road.
I stopped at the spot and looked at the broken divider.
There were shards of glass and a blood stain...
It was his.
The rain had failed to wash it away!

Open Manhole

The obnoxious odour of the drain
doesn't swirl in my memory,
it's the jeers of the crowd
that still ring in my ears.

— Nowhere Souls! —

Soulless souls
in a packed bus
jostle...get down,
melt into the crowd
and head towards an oblivion.

Paradise Of Pain

These futile frustrations,
outbursts of helplessness;
disenchanted desires, confused convictions;
shadows of mirages, unwept despair;
choked zest, sad realizations, forced lessons.

A heart sick of honesty,
lips tired with truth.
A bold integrity that leaves collective gasps.
The pooh-poohed commitments
and the unworthy worthlessness of an attainable perfection.
Where will I carry these with me?
Perhaps, into another hell that will never know
how my being was shaped in a paradise of pain.

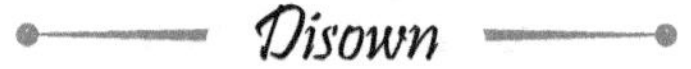 **Disown**

It is so hard to disclaim
what you have earned so assiduously.
The possessions that you have sacrificed a lifetime for
and bargained your sleep to attain.

Relinquishing them is tough, indeed.
But when you do so,
you take a baby step towards
striking a harmony with a deep-seated voice in you
that asks you: Do you really own anything?

Moving On...

Toxic ties,
Bland lies,
Subdued sighs,
Obscure whys!!

— No Gainers —

In this game of survival,
We all are losers.
The gains are actually
adding up to our miseries.

Hypocrisy Of Humans

The hypocrisy of being a human
and living in a civilized world
that borders on barbarism.

The farce of upholding rights
to save a guilty conscience
and getting pinned down every day
by exploitation of an ambition.

The hollowness of happiness
that hides an invisible abyss
and treasuring today's joys
that would be reduced to just a memory tomorrow.

The duplicity of emotions that can tie bonds
only till they last
and attachments that don't feel the warmth
despite constant connectivity.

The mockery of the mask
unable to conceal the secret
and camouflaging the faces
that hold up warped mirrors.

— Lies And Truth —

Lies of civilization stare
in the face of blindfolded truth.

Asthma

This development is breathtaking,
how it leaves us gasping for breath!

Slips

It was a regular day, but with some aberrations and slips.

My wife left the half-finished cup of tea
and hurried to catch her bus, as always,
except that she forgot her usual waving of the hand at me:
a gesture I had grown so accustomed to.

My son carried that burden on his shoulders
and rushed out of the room, like he always did
but he didn't bang the door behind him:
a noise that I had got so familiar with.

The elevator had been 'full'
and my steps moved towards the stairs as a routine.
Just that the lift reached the ground floor before me,
I lost the race that I had been winning till now.

The scooter needed seven kicks to start
and I could smell the belching smoke as I sat to drive
when I realized that something was missing:
the helmet that I could never do without.

The watchman at the gate was busy making some entry
and didn't greet me with that customary 'hello'.
I sped past him, without bothering to shift his attention
and offer him my feeble smile.

There were normal tailbacks;
I tried paving my way through the nightmarish traffic.
But encountered two cabbies trading punches on the road
and I punched in late.

Putting my bag near my office computer,
my hand reached into my pocket for the mobile phone.
I checked it, one unread message:
'Meet me asap'… it was my boss.

I thought it was about missing the deadline,
But it was another slip: the pink one.

Rift

I watch the storm blowing
that sweeps trust away
and flattens homes of harmony.

I watch the walls coming up;
the bricks of alienation,
mortar that cements hatred.

Reality

Obsession with progress
is not civilization
and fixation with longevity
is not life.

I looked at the clock;
its hands didn't move.
In its stillness,
I felt the pulse of a time gone by.

I kept my ears close to the wall.
The plaster peeling off it
told me stories of the myriad moments
I had spent to strengthen the bricks.

I touched the layers of dust on the AC
and wiped off the settled dirt,
Only to find a stifled memory
gliding in the air.

I chanced upon an outdated medicine;
Its pack reminded me of a disease
that has left behind
an incurable regret.

I glanced at the hanging calendar;
the dates seemed like a lost era;
I thought how dreams outlive age.
And passion becomes wise!

Pollution Of Pretension

We carry the
pollution of pretension
in our veins
and worry about the
toxicity that has seeped into
our actions
and become the lifeblood
of an existence removed from truth.

Minarets

When the Metro train passed by,
from a certain point
the four minarets appeared as two.
It then dawned on me
how we see things from a particular angle
and miss half the truth.

# Effort

In the effort to
build assets after assets,
life turns into a liability.

Aren't We All Migrants?

Sometimes, I wonder:
Aren't we all migrants?
Dislodged by destiny
from the home of our dreams,
We become refugees
in a world of strangers
trying to find a new house
which can shelter our secret desires,
Only to realize that
the only reality is homelessness
and desires can't keep pining for a lost abode.

Bitter

Bitter memories are like
non-biodegradable plastic bags.

They pile up, choke and pollute
the soil of our soul,
the ocean of our emotion.
They refuse to decompose
and stay there to torment
and suffocate us...

till we find an alternative
to get out of the contamination.

There's Nothing Wrong

There's nothing wrong if you occasionally forget
the name of the colleague sitting right next to you.
It doesn't mean you are oblivious or unsmart.

There's nothing wrong if you like a loud party with your friends
which goes into the wee hours.
It doesn't mean you can't appreciate solitude or discipline.

There's nothing wrong if you are filled with apathy
when you see TV channels churning out
the same TRP-driven gang rape news.
It doesn't mean you lack empathy or have lost the fire in your belly.

There's nothing wrong if you frustratedly chide your child
when the little one persistently throws tantrums
for an unaffordable stuff.
It doesn't mean you are uncaring or not a doting parent.

There's nothing wrong if you lose your cool over a snaking queue at
a supermarket counter
when you sense that your periods are on the verge.
It doesn't mean you don't have patience or are too finicky.

There's nothing wrong if you argue on buying
something for yourself
that you have been procrastinating endlessly
even when you know that it may need budgetary overhaul.
It doesn't mean you are being demanding or are inflexible.

There's nothing wrong if you are not able to keep your promise of
preparing your family's favourite dish due to a looming deadline.
It doesn't mean you don't value a vow or can't keep your word.

There's nothing wrong if you talk to your partner constantly on
your mobile phone
trying to convince your soulmate about your love.
It doesn't mean you are being weak or servile.

There's nothing wrong in crying alone in secret loneliness
but smile a smile that you don't own only to keep the game going.
It doesn't mean your effort is fake or hollow.

There's nothing wrong if even though you avoid
stepping on the ants
you squash those mosquitoes in fear of dengue.
It doesn't mean you are insensitive or don't believe in harmony.

There's nothing wrong in not offering prayers to God or
not chanting hymns
while helping that old woman carry her heavy bags
and share the burden.
It doesn't mean you lack respect for the divine,
for you love His beings.

Survivors?

We want to make ourselves believe
that we are out-and-out survivors.
But are we really?
Have we survived the battle absolutely?
Isn't a part of our soul already dead?
That part which was most vital: the core of our strength,
The part that can never be revived again.

Yes, we survive, but only just...

For Survival

How many deaths will you live through
to endure this stilted survival?

About the Author

Tirtho calls himself an international citizen and believes in *vasudhaiva kutumbakam* (the world is one family).

Tirtho has been a media professional for over two decades now. He has lived in several cities. Passionate about travelling to remote places, Tirtho doesn't lose a single opportunity to commune with nature.

This is his second book.